Praise
Mos

"Renee Raney is an award-winning environmental educator with a vast background in sharing her enthusiasm for nature, especially with respect to living in awareness of its importance. In her new book, she takes a reader's mind to new possibilities in understanding the visible and invisible worlds, and bridges reality and enchantment in ways that refresh and relax and stimulate wonder in the mind."

— Sherry Kughn, author of the Heart Tree Series for Empty Nesters

"The world needs more fairy houses, and more books like this one. *Hairy, Scary, but Mostly Merry Fairies!* will enchant young readers and is sure to inspire creativity in nature."

— Richard Louv, author of *Last Child in the Woods*

"Renee Raney's writing is captivating because it mixes the real world and the world of magic so seamlessly. I began seeing the glint of fairy dust in the woods outside my living room window while reading the first few pages of *Hairy, Scary, but Mostly Merry Fairies!*, and the spell was never broken. This book for young readers will have thousands of adult fans, and with very good reason. It's a masterpiece."

— Jordan Fisher Smith, author of *Engineering Eden*

"A great way of encouraging kids to get out and really look at their natural world. Renee Raney is a trained biologist and provides many fun and imaginative activities for teachers, kids, and parents to explore, write, draw, and build in their backyards, woods, or parks."

— Twig C. George, author of *Pocket Guide to the Outdoors*

"An enchanting book! *Hairy, Scary, but Mostly Merry Fairies!* helped me rediscover my belief in the fairy kingdom. Renee Raney's creative writing style will delight both children and adults. There is much in the book for nature lovers and to stimulate the imagination. Every public library—every person!—should have a copy."

— Elizabeth Cline, retired public librarian and fairy expert

"Renee Raney takes you on an enchanting journey into the realm of imagination. Her fairies lead children away from the sterile electronic world that has robbed so many of them of the creative joy of childhood. Children have not changed, if you introduce the world of fairies and dreams to them, they love it just as much as the generations who came before. This book gives us the tools we need to travel back into time when magic could teach us so much about reality."

— Verna Gates, Founder and Executive Director, Fresh Air Family

Hairy, Scary, but Mostly Merry Fairies!

Also by Renee Simmons Raney

Calico Ghosts

Hairy, Scary, but Mostly Merry Fairies!

Curing Nature Deficiency through Folklore, Imagination, and Creative Activities

RENEE SIMMONS RANEY

ILLUSTRATIONS BY CAROLYN WALKER CROWE

NEWSOUTH BOOKS
Montgomery

NewSouth Books
105 S. Court Street
Montgomery, AL 36104

 Published in the United States by NewSouth Books, a division of NewSouth, Inc., Montgomery, Alabama.

Publisher's Cataloging-in-Publication data

Raney, Renee Simmons.
Hairy, scary, but mostly merry fairies : curing nature deficiency through folklore, imagination, and creative activities /
Renee Simmons Raney ; illustrations by Carolyn Walker Crowe.
p. cm.

ISBN 978-1-58838-328-0 (paperback)
ISBN 978-1-60306-421-7 (ebook)

1. Fairies. 2. Fairies—Dwellings—Design and construction.
3. Fairies—Homes and haunts—Design and construction.
4. Nature craft. I. Title.

Library of Congress Control Number available upon request.

The illustrations for this book were inspired by Renee's stories and Victorian images of the wee folk, and were created by Renee's aunt, Carolyn Walker Crowe.

Design by Randall Williams

Manufactured by Thomson-Shore, Dexter, MI, USA; RMA150JM03, February, 2017

To Noseplips . . .

Every man's life is a fairy tale written by God's fingers.

— Hans Christian Andersen

When the first baby laughed for the first time, its laugh broke into a thousand pieces, and they all went skipping about, and that was the beginning of fairies.

— Peter Pan

If you want your children to be intelligent, read them fairy tales. If you want them to be more intelligent, read them more fairy tales.

— Albert Einstein

Let the little fairy in you fly!

— Rufus Wainwright

Contents

You can understand and relate to most people better if you look at them—no matter how old or impressive they may be—as if they are children. For most of us never really grow up or mature all that much—we simply grow taller. O, to be sure, we laugh less and play less and wear uncomfortable disguises like adults, but beneath the costume is the child we always are, whose needs are simple, whose daily life is still best described by fairy tales.

— Leo Rosten

Once Upon a Time

. . . which is really the only decent way to begin a fairy tale, there was a little girl named Renee. She was born from a prayer and a wish. Her mother is Swiss-Irish. Her father is Scotch-Cherokee. She was raised on a mystical dairy farm. She spoke to the animals, interacted with the fairy folk, and learned to respect even the tiniest portions of the natural world. Most people lose touch with the enchantment . . . but not her. As she grew up, she learned to share the magic with others.

Hairy, Scary, but Mostly Merry Fairies!

Where the bee sucks, there suck I;
In a cowslip's bell I lie;
There I couch when owls do cry.
On the bat's back I do fly
After summer merrily.
Merrily, merrily shall I live now
Under the blossom that hangs on the bough.

— William Shakespeare

1

First Sighting

THE CLOUDS ABOVE ME were white shifting shapes moving slowly across the spring sky. The calico patchwork quilt underneath me was warm from the sun. I lay stretched on my back. My best friend, Nosy, the little black dog, lay beside me like a guardian. I felt safe, loved, and completely content.

In the distance I could hear the electric milking machine in Granddad's dairy barn—chicka-chug, chicka-chug, chicka-chug—as it pulled the milk from our beautiful Holstein cows and piped it into the ice-cold milk tanks. Every now and then Granddad would sing along with the radio. His voice was a little off-key, but so full of "happy" that it made me smile.

Nearer to my nest, I could hear the buzzing of honeybees as they bumbled from blossom to blossom collecting pollen. I loved to watch the bees. They seemed so focused on their task that I'm sure they weren't aware of a big world chaotically chicka-chugging around them.

My world was bigger than the bees' but small enough that I felt like the princess of a perfectly adorable kingdom. The entire farm ranged over a hundred acres—the "Hundred Acre Wood" we called it, after Winnie-the-Pooh. But the core of my world was the ten acres surrounding Nonnie and Granddad's farm cottage. I knew every nook and cranny. I was friends with every growing thing, every creeping thing, every crawling thing, and especially the birds and bugs. I had an innate sense that the Creator had endowed me with a duty and responsibility to take care of these little creatures.

A large green dragonfly hovered over my quilt. He seemed to nod his head as if to acknowledge my presence. I waved a hand at him in greeting and he zipped away.

The bees were buzzing quite loudly and there was birdsong, but along with those sounds was a new one, a kind of buzz-hum, almost like a bumblebee humming rather than buzzing. I sat up on the quilt. Nosy's ears perked up as she looked toward the odd noise. It seemed to be coming from the base of the old white oak tree that grew in the sparse Breezy Woods next to my meadow. I tippy-tiptoed toward the tree, taking my time and moving silently as Daddy had taught me: "Cherokee walk heel to toe when they move through the wood . . . slowly . . . to make no noise." Nosy followed discreetly behind.

I stood statue-still, becoming part of the wood, as my eyes and mind registered what was making the sound. There, at the twisted above-ground roots of the oak tree, was— I knew it!! I knew they were real even though I'd never seen one. I'd found their footprints and other evidence. I'd seen them out of the corner of my eyes, but here, in plain view, was a FAIRY!

He was standing with his back to me, his hands on his hips with elbows out as if he were challenging the tree. The iridescent wings on his back were folded downward like those of a resting damselfly. He was dressed in brown except for a tiny orange hat. As I watched, he gathered three acorn caps (which to him was a full armload) and spread his wings. With a hummmm, he flew off toward the field.

I walked to the base of the tree for a closer look. I realized a chipmunk was hiding in a little knothole next to a root. He was pushing out empty acorn caps from inside the tree. He hadn't noticed me, so again I became part of the woods and watched.

The chipmunk disappeared inside the tree for a few seconds and then reappeared, pushing three acorn caps at a time out of the hole. Then he would carefully stack the caps on the edge of the gnarled old root and return inside to repeat the process.

I eased to my knees to blend in with the fragrant honeysuckle vines growing next to the oak. Nosy squatted next to me as we waited. We were close enough to see the expression of joy on the little

chipmunk's face as he peered toward the treetops. He looked as if he was expecting another visit. Sure enough, we heard the buzz-humm sound, faintly at first, then it grew louder. The same brown fairy zipped down from the sky and stood at the base of the tree. He pointed at the six acorn caps as if counting them, reached into the tiny pouch at his side, pulled out seeds of some sort, and laid them in front of the knothole. The chipmunk smiled at the fairy, put all the seeds in his furry "chipmunky" cheeks and went back inside the tree.

The fairy disappeared with three of the caps and then quickly returned for the other three. He buzzed a little too close to us on his last flight out and Nosy barked at him. He was so close that I saw a startled look on his beautiful little face as he realized he had an audience. He dropped one of the acorn caps in his haste to zigzag away from us.

I sat still for what seemed hours. I hoped he'd return for the dropped cap so that I might see him again. When it became apparent that he wasn't coming back, I picked up the tiny object. What had appeared to be a regular acorn cap was actually a tiny work of art. Obviously, the chipmunk was friend or pet to another fairy who lived deep within the oak tree and manufactured acorn-cap fairy dishes. The little cap had been slightly reshaped so that when turned upside down it sat perfectly like a little bowl. Some dainty artist had carved clever patterns in the sides of the little bowl. Obviously, the brown fairy was trading seeds or grain for these little dishes.

I wanted to keep the little acorn cap, but I knew I hadn't paid for it or earned it. So I put it back on the root where the fairy had picked up the other dishes. I heard the chipmunk fussing at me from inside the hole so I moved away quickly. I thought perhaps after Nosy and I left that the fairy would return and find his lost dish. Perhaps he'd understand that I wanted to be his friend.

I ran to the farm cottage and told Nonnie what I'd heard, seen, and done. I thought she'd laugh at me or just assume I was playing another of my imagination games. But she didn't. She began to tell me stories of fairies she'd seen when she was a young girl. She said that not all people can see fairies. Nonnie was very happy that I could! She promised to teach me to build fairy houses and other wonderful things about these secretive little creatures.

The next morning, I went back to the old oak tree. The acorn-cap was gone and in its place was a tiny bouquet of "bluet" flowers tied with a tiny red string: a symbol of thanks from the fairy for not stealing the bowl. Nonnie said that I had taken the first step to making friends with the wee folk. I tucked the little bouquet in my wishing book along with my collection of pressed four-leaf clovers.

And as the seasons come and go,
here's something you might like to know.
There are fairies everywhere:
under bushes, in the air,
playing games just like you play,
singing through their busy day.
So listen, touch, and look around
in the air and on the ground.
And if you watch all nature's things,
you might just see a fairy's wing.

— Author Unknown

It's easy to believe in magic when you're young. Anything you couldn't explain was magic then. It didn't matter if it was science or a fairy tale. Electricity and elves were both infinitely mysterious and equally possible—elves probably more so.

— Charles de Lint

Some day you will be old enough to start reading fairy tales again.

— C. S. Lewis

2

The Natural History of Fairies

NONNIE TOLD ME ALL OF the fairy stories that she knew from when she was a little girl. Then we visited our public library to borrow several books on fairies. I discovered so many things about them by reading old legends and folk lore from Ireland, Scotland, and England. When you want to learn about something, read!! Books are a wonderful resource for finding out what is true and what isn't. But don't just stop there . . . read and investigate! Explore and experiment so that what you read doesn't just stay in your mind, but becomes part of your memory as an experience.

The stories reported many interesting facts. I learned that fairies can come in all shapes, sizes and colors. Some are so tiny that the human eye can't see them. Some are so large that we wouldn't recognize them as fairies. Some can fly. Some are earthbound. Some are invisible. Some are fast and others are slow. I realized that most common fairies like to live near old oak trees, like to hold their dances beneath willow trees, and that I should

beware of mushrooms growing in a circle. A circle of mushrooms is called a fairy ring. One who accidentally stands in the center of a fairy ring risks being kidnapped by the prince of fairies. It sounds like an adventure; however, the prince may keep his human for a thousand years. I realized that I would NOT like to be away from my farm and wood for a thousand years!

I learned from my observation of the first fairy that he collected bluets, the tiny blue-lavender flowers that grow on my farm. You wouldn't notice bluets from a standing position. You have to lean down close to the ground or even crawl on your hands and knees to find patches of them. It took four days, but I found a patch of bluets growing near the "Grandpop Tree," which was our name for a hundred-year-old chestnut oak that nestled wisely between two sedge-covered rises in the large field. I thought about camouflaging myself and hiding near the bluet patch to wait on my fairy. Then I realized that I couldn't really hide myself from a fairy. Wouldn't you notice an elephant in your living room? Reasonably, the best approach would be a simple and truthful one.

I sat down on a giant oak tree root. I was very still and quiet. I sat patiently for a long time. I didn't mind waiting because I had my imagination with me. I pretended all sorts of wonderful things in my mind while my eyes stayed focused on the bluet patch. After several hours I was rewarded for my diligence. There among the small flowers I saw movement—three fairies appeared and began to pick bluets, placing them in little baskets. These fairies appeared to be females, and they were dressed in pastel colors. The fairy colors are difficult to describe, like the pale pearl gray in the ring around the moon or the peachy purple streak of a setting sun. They were beautiful.

I didn't approach them. I sat and studied them from my root seat. I knew they saw me, for every now and again they would glance over at me. When their baskets were filled with flowers, they spread iridescent wings that were like the rainbow sheen of a bubble and flew away.

After observing fairies doing all sorts of marvelous simple things, I realized that I was what the old Irish tales called *fey*, or "fairy aware." Not everyone is fey; you are born with this gift as some are born to be musicians or artists. I love music and art, but I cannot create it the way gifted musicians and artists can. Similarly, many people love fairies and enchanting stories, but they just can't see them.

Being fey, I was able to discern enchantment. This meant that as I was walking along a path or wandering through a wood, I could detect fairy glamour. I would feel the enchantment wash over my face like a cool breeze. My eyes would automatically search out a spot where the fairies might live, work or play. Because of this, I began to see more fairies than I could have ever imagined. Sometimes I would glimpse them out of the corner of my eye. Or sometimes I would focus on them in that "in between" space, like when you look at one thing, letting your eyes relax, and then you see everything.

If you are fey, you will know what I mean. If you

aren't, you can pretend to be fey simply by using your imagination! Some people say that every child is born fey, but they lose faith in the unseen world as they grow older. I thought it was rare to find fey adults, but there are many more of us than I ever dreamed!

I LOVE TO WANDER in the mountains and to hike the deep canyons of the Cumberland Gap and Appalachian Mountains. Many tumbling rivers have created enchanted gorges full of boulders, endangered species . . . and myths and legends.

One of my favorite legends is that of the Little People who were called Yunwi Tsunsdi (pronounced Yun-wee Joon-stee) by the Cherokee Indians who first populated this region. These Little People are "nature spirits." They can render themselves invisible but usually manifest as small, child-like humans. When threatened or angry, they sprout thick rough hair all over their faces and their teeth become long and sharp. They live in rock caves along the river, and their purpose is to defend the waters to keep them safe for creatures who live there.

The Little People are tricksters. Many hikers become lost in the forest because the Little People have placed an enchantment on them or have altered the trails. It is said the Little People can read human intent very easily. Therefore, if you are a kind person, they will treat you kindly. But if you are an unkind person, they will trick you and lead you astray.

I have never met a Yunwi Tsunsdi face to face. But I have been hiking along the river and heard splashing water. When I investigated, there was no one to be seen, but there were child-sized wet footprints all over the boulders and in one spot, water dripping from an invisible source about twelve inches high. When I laughed and said, "Osiho Dohitsu," which means "Hello, how are you?" in Cherokee, there was a mischievous laugh in response and I was splashed from all around by invisible tiny hands. This sparkling-laughing-splashing of water traveled across the river away from me and disappeared into the forest.

My Scotch-Cherokee father told me that when he was a young boy he became lost in the woods late one evening. He wasn't frightened, but he knew his mother would worry if he wasn't home by dark. He built a small fire on a sandy spot of soil, careful to clear any debris away first. He spread out on a big green leaf by the fire a few crackers that he had in his pocket.

He closed his eyes and sang a song that his grandfather had taught him to sing when one needs help in the forest. When he finished singing, he opened his eyes. The crackers were gone and there, by the fire, a map was drawn in the sand. The Little People understood his song. They knew he was a good person, accepted his meal offering, and directed him home.

"Just living is not enough" said the butterfly fairy,
"One must have sunshine, freedom and a little flower."

— Hans Christian Andersen

Believe in the Fairies
Who make dreams come true.
Believe in the wonder,
The stars and the moon.
Believe in the magic,
From Fairies above.
They dance on the flowers,
And sing songs of love.
And if you just believe,
And always stay true,
The Fairies will be there,
To watch over you!

— Author unknown

3

Fairy Houses

I REALIZED THAT ONCE fairy folk are discovered they are swift to move on to hide themselves from humans. The chipmunk den where I had seen the little brown fairy—my first—was vacated soon after my encounter with him. I knew this from paying close attention and observing the area. The entrance became overgrown with unkempt weeds. A spider built her web over the opening and this let me know that there was no coming to or going from that place.

Nonnie said they wouldn't have moved very far from that location; just far enough to become invisible again. She said that the best thing we could do was to build some fairy houses in the area to let them know that we were friends and not invaders. She also warned me not to bring too many other humans around the area. Fairies tend to leave if too many humans are aware of a natural space and less desirable creatures like trolls and gnurls (gnomes gone bad) show up, causing all sorts of chaos.

I learned that fairy houses are traditional in Ireland, Scotland, and England. In Cottingley, England, two young girls (Elsie Wright and Frances Griffiths) built fairy houses and photographed their fairy friends in a secret forest near their home. Sir Arthur Conan Doyle (you may remember him as the author of *The Adventures of Sherlock Holmes*) believed Elsie's and Frances's stories. He wrote an article for *The Strand* newspaper in November 1920, with two of the fairy photos printed for the world to view.

Some believed in these fairies and others did not. I have heard that too many human visitors explored the area searching for evidence. This offended the fairies who departed on wing, foot, and leaf boats. The enchanted forest became "just another woodland" until the fairies felt it was safe to return.

This has been on my mind as I write this book. What if too many people read it and cause problems for the fairies? But I plan to seek permission from the Prince of Fairies before I publish this manuscript. I truly believe that he will place just enough fairy glamour on this book to ensure that only the RIGHT kind of people read it—those who will have respect for the enchanted world and who will not cause any problems for the fairy folk.

Besides, the Prince has told me countless times that the fairies need more fairy houses . . . many of them. The natural places are not as abundant as they once were, so restful little dens of habitation make life much easier on the fairies, especially those who work daily to help trees and animals.

ANYONE CAN BUILD A fairy house. The main tool needed is imagination. Pretend that you are only about three inches tall. This would be the same size as your pointy finger. Where would you like to live? What would you want to see from your house? What might attract you to a special location? Is it near a creek? Are mushrooms or mosses or partridge berry vines growing there?

The second tool is observation. You must look around in your yard, in the woods, in the fields, or on the beach. Wherever you are, you can spot an ideal location for a fairy house. You may want to build it on the ground, in a tree, or by the roots of a tree. Get down on your knees and look closely at the ground. Climb up a tree and look around at the world. Fairies are as different from one another as humans, but all tend to be attracted to homes that meet their basic needs with lovely view, shelter, food and water.

The only rule is to use natural materials so that we do not disturb the habitat of the area. Fairies shy away from most man-made or unnatural objects. Some children place glitter in and around their fairy houses. Please don't. Fairies are allergic to glitter and will not come near the stuff!

To begin, I usually collect ten to twenty sticks

that I can break into smaller pieces. These will become walls, ceilings, steps, and ladders. Pine cones, hickory nuts, acorns, and other objects make excellent decorations. Remember that if you are in a park or on public lands it is illegal to pick anything that is growing, so if you desire flowers to be part of your fairy house, build the house where flowers are growing. You can also use flowers from a greenhouse or a flower shop. Fairies love real flower blossoms.

Never move large objects like rocks or logs. You can build your fairy house next to a log or a large rock, but remember that log and that large rock are already a home to thousands of creatures. The fairies do not want us to damage our natural world.

Building fairy houses is an excellent way to observe nature. Many times I have observed other creatures visiting the fairy houses that I've built. I've seen crickets, ladybugs, yellow jackets, butterflies, field mice, carpenter ants, spiders, toads, frogs, birds, and even a bat! Some people will say these creatures simply were attracted to the new little habitat space provided for them. But I know better.

After years of observing fairies on our farm, in the deep woods of national forests, along the cliffs of canyons, in aspen groves in the Rocky Mountains, on sandy beaches, along the rocky coasts of Maine, Oregon, and Washington, in the mists beneath the giant Redwoods, in the rain forests of Puerto Rico, on the snowy cliffs of Canada, in the becks of Ireland, and everywhere in between, I've realized that the fairies communicate with wildlife. Oftentimes when one sees a creature in his or her fairy house, that creature has been sent by the fairies to observe the structure. That little creature will report back to the fairies as to whether the house is worth visiting.

Creatures love to hear stories and songs. So, as I build my fairy houses, I tell stories (very quietly). The creatures will take the stories back to the fairy children and repeat them. Just as we tell fairy tales to our human children, fairies tell human tales to their fairy children! Where do they get these tales? By sending out their creature spies to listen, of course! Didn't Peter Pan ask Wendy, "Do you know why swallows build in the eaves of houses?"

And didn't he answer, "It is to listen to the stories."

Two types of birds, wrens and phoebes, spend much of their time building nests on porches or in flower pots—basically as close as they can get to human families. These birds listen to our stories, prayers, conversations, and songs. Often they fairy-sit young fairies in their nests and, if you've built fairy habitations near your garden, they will bring the little fairy children to play there.

When I was a child, I built fairy houses all over the Breezy Woods where I had seen my first fairy. I built them beneath the Grandpop Tree. I built them in the crooked branches of the twisted willows. Sometimes the houses would seem uninhabited for days. Sometimes fairies never visited. Sometimes they visited, but the only evidence was that they ate the tiny banquet (seeds, bread crumbs, fruit) I had set out for them and they shifted things around. The best visits were the rare times when fairies left a token of appreciation behind. These tokens ranged from tiny bouquets of flowers, to strange coins, to

carved wooden animals and many other wonderful gifts which I have in my fairy collection. I keep these in a box and show them to participants at my Fairy House Workshops.

I taught my sons, Josh and Jo, to build fairy houses. We built them in our front yard and in our woods. We built them when we traveled across the United States throughout Alabama, Maine, Tennessee, Georgia, North Carolina, Colorado, Montana, Wyoming, California, and Washington. We've built them in other countries such as Ireland, Mexico, and Canada! An interesting note: We built a fairy house on the cliffs of Acadia National Park. When we went back seven years later, that house was still there. Other visitors had kept it up, added to it, and it was a splendid fairy castle!

Those of us who build fairy houses have learned that if we don't expect anything from the fairies, and if we built the house out of sheer joy and love of the wee folks, the fairies will usually visit.

I believe humans have innate enchantment and a love for nature deep in our souls. If we create fairy houses and fairy lures (whimsical objects hanging from trees to point the way to a fairy house) while tapping into that enchantment, the fairies and their creature friends can feel it. They are drawn faster to the houses that are built from belief than to houses that may be built with doubt or selfishness. If there is one thing that fairies dislike about humans, it is our selfish and sometimes greedy ways.

So when you build your own fairy houses, build them with love and care as if you were going to live there.

Soft moss a downy pillow makes,
and green leaves spread a tent,
Where Faerie fold may rest and sleep
until their night is spent.
The bluebird sings a lullaby,
the firefly gives a light,
The twinkling stars are candles bright,
Sleep, Faeries all, Good Night.

— Elizabeth T. Dillingham,
"A Faery Song"

If I had influence with the good fairy who is supposed to preside over the christening of all children, I should ask that her gift to each child in the world be a sense of wonder so indestructible that it would last throughout life.

— Rachel Carson

4

Seasonal Fairies

MOST FAIRIES LIVE IN shifts and perform seasonal work, taking turns at earth care and such. When they are not working, they either hibernate or migrate depending upon their specialties.

I've only caught one fairy. It was a complete accident, of course! By trade, I am a biologist or naturalist. I enjoy all aspects of nature observation. When I was in college I focused on learning everything I could about mammals, reptiles, amphibians, and birds, and their habitats. I took several ecology classes with a marvelously enchanted professor who was also fey: I will refer to him as "Dr. W." He had read much of C. S. Lewis's work and I suspect that Dr. W may have visited Narnia at least once in his life. Many of our classes were spent out in the field researching and observing the different species, how they behave and how they are connected to others. Dr. W would often stop and point to a mist of fog rising on a hill and say, "Do you see the fairy smoke?" He would point to a tree that had grown with a hole through the middle. With human eyes, we could look through the hole and see the forest on the other side of the tree. He would say, "If we were fairy-sized we could pass through that hole and enter a whole new world."

One spring I traveled to Alabama's Dauphin Island to observe the migration of birds. There were four of us working as ornithologists (scientists who study birds) on this island. As part of our work, we set up a mist net. These are fine-meshed nets that are spread between two poles. Birds fly into the nets and are caught but not harmed. We would gently hold the captured bird, weigh it, measure it, and place a tiny band around its leg for future

identification. If it were an interesting specimen, we'd photograph it. Then we would release it to fly away with an exciting story to tell its friends.

With the help of several bird-loving volunteers, I had captured and banded about fifty birds. We were done for the day and it was my turn to take down the nets for the night. Just as the others disappeared toward our research station, something very small flew into the net and stuck there with its wings humming. I thought it was a hummingbird. As I approached the little creature I realized that this was no bird. It was a fairy! Several of our volunteers were still out and about. I was terrified that someone would notice the new catch and come running to help. All of the researchers were great people, but, most were as "un-fey" as one can be. They would want to keep the little fellow—I could just imagine him captured in a jar with scientists staring and poking at him.

I quickly covered my eyes with my hands and whispered toward the sky a simple poem that Nonnie had taught me. This was similar to a "secret password" between fairy folk and fey folk. It was to let him know that I was a friend. Sorry, I can't repeat the poem here lest you use it irresponsibly, but if you ever come to one of my fairy house workshops and prove yourself to be a fairy friend, I will teach it to you.

He was mossy green and quite angry at being caught. His cicada-like wings buzzed and clicked as he tried to pull himself out of the net. After I spoke, he became still, but his sparkling little eyes looked at me warily from beneath his ruby-red cap.

I carefully untangled him from the mist net and set him on the table, where he seemed to relax a bit. He took a moment to catch his breath. He stretched out one foot and shook it. He stretched out the other foot and shook it. He raised his arms high and stretched. He opened his wings and closed them. Then he put his hands on his hips and grinned at me.

With an odd accent that sounded a bit like old Irish, he said, "Many thanks for your help. It is a rare thing to find fey folk in these times. If one must be caught in a snare, one appreciates the snare being manned by a believer."

Since he had spoken first, I knew that I could now speak directly to him. To speak first to a fairy is unthinkable and all sorts of ill luck might befall one so foolish!

ONE FEELS THE ENCHANTMENT of the coastal islands, especially near the shell mounds where the ancient live oaks droop their limbs to the ground in massive displays of majestic tree-ness. The live oak dryads (tree spirits) are graceful and strong. But I hadn't seen a single fairy while I was there. So my first question was, "Do you live on the island?"

He shook his small head and said, "No. I'm an avifairy. I migrate north with the ruby-throated hummingbirds in the spring and I fly south with them in the winter. I scout along the routes helping them locate food, shelter, and safety. In the spring I spend most of me time guarding nests and helping the young songbirds learn to fly. If a fledgling is lost, I help it find its mother. I was scouting out a safe route through this bramble when I was caught in your net. Now I must away or fall far behind my flock. Twalah!"

And he was gone.

Twalah is a word known only to fairy and fairy friends; it means hello and goodbye. If you suspect your friend is fey, you can greet them with "Twalah!" and if they are, they'll answer back. If not, they will usually ask, "What did you just say?"

From that day I spent a good deal of time observing the seasonality and specialty of fairy work. I've seen avi-fairies in the spring watching my hummingbird feeders. Once I saw one of these scouts swoop down, pick up a large praying mantis that had hidden near the feeder, and fly away. Another time, my fey Aunt Jenny told me that she watched three furry gray "mouse-like" fairies hang a bell on her cat's collar while he was sleeping in the sun, to keep him from sneaking up on birds.

Summer fairies are especially wild and gypsy-like. These are the fairies most often observed by children, because the children are outside on warm days and warm nights. Summer fairies spend most of their days herding honeybees to and from their hives. They drink honeysuckle nectar. To us it is just a sweet drop on the tongue, but to a small fairy it is like mead and can set them "drunk" very quickly. Intoxicated fairies are funny to watch, but don't let them know you see them. Fairies do not like to be laughed at unless they trying to be funny.

In the summer, one often hears the sweet gentle music of the fairy folk. It sounds something like wind chimes. Sometimes it sounds like the wind singing in the treetops. Other times it is a faint drumming, as if the woods themselves had a pulse. Fairies love to dance, so when you build a summer fairy house, be sure to build it large enough for several fairies to move about. One of my students was wise enough to build the fairies an amphitheater where they could have performances on a star-shaped stage and dance on a mossy courtyard.

Oftentimes I have sat on my front porch just as the sun was setting and watched summer fairies ride the little brown bats that swoop and circle over our front yard. It must be something like a rodeo for the fairies, because they fly toward the bat in a wild chase and then straddle the bat just above the wings, holding onto the bat's ears for a wild ride. Nothing is quite as magical as hearing those little summer fairies laugh as they are jolted about on a bat's back!

I learned a neat trick from a summer fairy that lived under my front steps and kept a toad as a pet. This little fairy would fly out each night and return with a firefly under each arm. The toad would hop out to greet him. The fairy would feed the fireflies to the toad and we'd watch the toad's throat and belly light up! It was enchanting.

As the trees begin to change their leaf color, the summer fairies all go to a raft (or underground fairy city) where they sleep for a season. The autumn fairies then begin to appear. These are the most diverse of all the fairies. They include the leaf fairies, who help the trees shed for winter; the harvest fairies, who help the earth produce its autumn fruits; the Halloween fairies, who are extremely mischievous and only come out for the thirteen days surrounding All Hallows Eve; and the "Go Between" fairies, who help the wild creatures store food for the winter.

The dances, wild rituals, and mystical music of the autumn fairies can border on the dangerous. Often these dancing wee folk can create fairy tornados that whisk along through yards and over fields, tossing leaves and dust to and fro. Other times their wings beat so quickly to the rhythm of the music that they begin to burn like coals in a fire. If a flaming fairy gets too close to a dry tree or patch of grass, it can cause a wild fire. If you see smoke boiling up from a deep forest in the autumn, know that it must be the location of a fairy "ceilli" (pronounced "kay-lee" and meaning fairy party).

If provoked, fairies of any season can be dangerous, mostly bringing bad luck to the offender. But if you hear the music of the autumn fairies, you'll never be the same. No matter how lovely the other seasons are, you'll long for autumn, when you'll be known to wander about—gallivant, even—through the woods and fields, with no particular destination or reason except to greet each colorful leaf and tree as if they are old friends. You may even find yourself having conversations with chipmunks and chickadees.

The autumn fairies also tend to borrow items from our homes. If a fairy borrows items from your

home, uses them for a bit, and brings them back, these things will be forever enchanted.

My lovely fey mother has a unique gift. She can sense fairy glamor on inanimate objects. For example, fairies borrowed several of our silver spoons. When these spoons returned, they were never quite the same. In the bubbly sink, as they waited to be washed, these spoons would quarrel with my mother, saying "Why did you wash the fork next? It was my turn!" Or when we would set the table, these spoons would make requests as to whom they would serve. Sometimes in the middle of the night we would hear these spoons singing moonlight songs to the other silverware.

"When I was in my cradle, a wood woman, a Dryad, spoke this verse over me: 'Where sky and water meet, Where the waves grow sweet, Doubt not, Reepicheep, To find all you seek, There is the utter East.' I do not know what it means. But the spell of it has been on me all my life."

— C. S. Lewis (Reepicheep, *Voyage of the Dawn Treader*)

5

Dryads

Most people think all fairies are extremely small. Fairies come in all sizes. I met several fairies who live their lives as HUMANS! One calls herself "Mrs. Cline" and pretends to be a librarian and a grandmother. The other is named "Elizabeth" and pretends to be a high school student. If you look closely at their eyes and ears, you would have no doubt that neither lady is a common mortal.

Some fairies are quite large, especially the dryads or tree spirits. These are among my favorite fairy spirits. They are reclusive and few people are fortunate enough to see them. It takes much patience and much desire to see a dryad.

The first dryad I encountered was the spirit of an oakleaf hydrangea bush growing near the edge of my grandfather's orchard. I love to walk in the moonlight and look around at the world. Everything looks so different by moonlight. I was walking by moonlight through the orchard during the late summer of my eighth human year when, far ahead of me, I saw a lovely old woman sitting on a stool. She was knitting something very carefully as she would lean down to look closely at her hands and then look up and smile at the moon. The moon would smile back and the lady would continue to knit. She had silvery white hair. She was dressed in leafy garments. As I slowly approached, she folded her knitting tightly to her chest, smiled at me lovingly and turned back into the oakleaf hydrangea.

I ran back to my little cottage and found my daddy. I told him what I had seen and he said I was very fortunate. I had seen the hydrangea's dryad working by moonlight. He said all trees have spirits and some are more industrious than others. Just like people . . . some work hard, some barely work, others play hard, and yet others have forgotten how to play.

The next day I visited the hydrangea by daylight. She was a lovely bush covered in white blossoms which were beginning to dry out into lace. I found several black swallowtail butterfly chrysalises hanging from her limbs. She must have knitted the little cocoons for the butterflies in the moonlight. Later I found out that many of the smaller fairies use the discarded silky cocoons of moths and butterflies as bassinets for their fairy babies.

I've seen willow tree dryads dance together around the edges of the marsh. I've walked hand-in-limb beside the dryad of a tulip poplar tree and listened to wisdom beyond height or depth. Dryads are the most compassionate and forgiving of all the sprites. For example, they understand that people need wood from trees to survive. As long as trees are harvested with respect and in moderation, they don't mind. When a tree is taken, the dryad simply

moves into another seedling and begins its life cycle over. They love humans and all creatures because they understand that our breath is their lifeline. Humans just need to remember that it works both ways—without the trees and plants we'd have no breath for life. The Creator made sure that everything is connected.

The evergreen trees play host for winter fairies and creatures that don't migrate. Evergreen dryads are extremely jolly; you can usually tell when one passes by because you will get a whiff of their spicy fragrance. The longleaf pine trees host unique fairies who not only care for the giant fire-dependent cones but also for the endangered red-cockaded woodpeckers who make their nest cavities in the living longleaf trees. These evergreen fairies never sleep.

But when the last leaves drop from the non-evergreen trees, like maples and oaks, the deciduous dryads sink far down into the depths of their respective trees to sleep for the winter. They wake up in the spring to assist their trees with leaf growing, but they rarely exit their trees at that time because waking up is much more difficult than falling asleep.

Some dryads need a wee bit more respect than others because they tend to be quite temperamental. These are the spirits that inhabit carnivorous plants.

They are the guardians of unique habitats where many endangered species make a home.

Once I had the misfortune to observe a boy tormenting a frog in the river by poking it with a stick. Before I could intervene on behalf of the frog, one of the protected carnivorous green pitcher plants growing nearby lifted its roots from the sandy soil, stalked over to stand behind the boy, dropped its "mouth or pitcher" shaped leaf over the boys head and sucked him in like a spaghetti noodle!

I gasped with surprise, and the plant made a little growl, shivered, spit the boy's tennis shoes onto the river bank, and returned to its original spot on the shore. A few hours later, the boy washed up on the sandy bank downstream. He was barefoot but unharmed and said he would never poke a frog "or any living creature" with a stick ever-ever-ever again!

To this day, when I hike along the river and see unclaimed shoes scattered along the banks, I remember how this ferocious little plant taught a naughty boy an important lesson.

When the winds of March are wakening
the crocuses and crickets,
Did you ever find a fairy near some
budding little thickets, . . .
And when she sees you creeping up
to get a closer peek
She tumbles through the daffodils,
a playing hide and seek.

— Marjorie Barrows

6

Holiday Fairies

THERE ARE VARIOUS FAIRIES associated with most major human holidays and there are fairy holidays that humans are not aware of. Here I will discuss several types.

ALL SPICE EVE

On All Spice Eve, the wild autumn fairies and the deciduous tree dryads gather on Harvest Moon night for a festive dance. The fairies drink the fermented flower nectar of the last flowers and become intoxicated. The music they create would cause a mortal to start dancing and never stop. This symphony is filled with drums and flutes which cause the dryads to form a fiery ballet. It is a feral and magical night for the fairies. As they spin and twirl beneath the autumn canopy, their wings heat up and begin to glow like the embers of a fire. Golden dust spews from their wings and floats down to earth to become spices such as cinnamon, nutmeg, ginger, and clove. The air is filled with the fragrance of these spices and the scent wafts through the forests, over the meadows, and even into towns. If you are outside admiring the Harvest Moon, breathe deeply and see if you can catch a whiff of the autumn fairy spices! The Forest Service fire team (including Smoky Bear) goes on special alert during this time because these fairies become so wild that they sometimes accidentally set the woods on fire!

Halloween

Halloween is an important fairy time. They celebrate for thirteen days that culminate on All Hallows Eve in one big event all over the world. I've started making at least one fairy house out of a jack-o'-lantern and so far it has been inhabited by fairies each time.

You might find wild rogue fairies in a farmer's pumpkin patch. These mischievous wee folk make pumpkin moonshine beneath the vines, and you can smell the odd scent as you walk along the pumpkin meadow. The wings of these fairies look like luna moth wings. You may see them flitting around the streetlamp or the light on your front porch catching insects for their pet bats. Others have no wings at all and ride black cats. If you have a black cat and it begins to act oddly around Halloween, you can be assured that a fairy has adopted said cat and is training it.

One of the strangest sights is to look up at the October moon and see a "witch riding a broomstick across the orb." Halloween fairies love to play tricks on mortals and one trick is that a flighted fairy will pick up a branch with a frayed edge and fly across the moon while cackling with laughter.

Many graveyard fairies enjoy the Halloween season. The graveyard fairies are small gray skeletal-looking beings with long, bony fingers who watch for mortals to drive or walk through a cemetery. These wee folks create strange mists, eerie fog, ephemeral lights, and odd noises to frighten humans away from their villages that are built deep in the roots of old oak and ancient cedar trees.

CHRISTMAS

There are so many types of Christmas fairies—Woodland Fairies, Santa Claus and his twin brother Krampuss, Christmas Tree Fairies, Nativity Fairies, and more.

Woodland Fairies spend most mornings and evenings feeding winter creatures and taking care of little animals that get lost in the cold. These fairies work during the other seasons filling up their storehouses with grain, berries, nuts, and seeds. They hide the bounty in hollow logs, knotholes of trees, and underground so that food will be plentiful during the lean, cold, snowy winter months.

Some fairies are extremely musical and they can

train families of field mice to sing Christmas carols for their festivals.

Santa Claus is known as a jolly old man who rewards good children with presents and goodies in their Christmas stockings. Not many people know about his twin brother, Krampuss. Krampuss is the mischievous elf—perhaps we should call him a goblin—who puts chunks of coal and switches in the naughty children's stockings. In Europe children are warned that if they continue to be bad after Krampuss warns them, the next year he will pop them into his big bag and turn them into cookies! Santa rewards children for being unselfish and loving. Krampuss helps to keep children from being greedy and spoiled.

Christmas Tree Fairies are actually Evergreen Fairies. When a living Christmas tree is cut from where it grows, the evergreen dryad simply moves onto the seed and begins life in another tree. But the fairies that were living in the evergreen branches hide themselves until the tree is decorated. Then, as the lights are turned on, the fairies use their glamour to make the tree magical and special. Children and pets often see the Christmas Tree Fairies playing hide-and-seek among the ornaments. Cats often get in trouble with their owners for diving into a Christmas tree to chase a fairy round about! The fairies think it is tremendous fun to tease the kitty, for they are much too fast to ever be caught by a house cat.

Nativity Fairies are descended from a feather dropped from the wing of an angel who flew over the Christ Child's manger. Legends have told us that when the feather swirled above the baby Jesus, he gave his first human laugh, and the laugh sparked up into the night sky as a giant star. After a few nights, the star began to shatter into hundreds of tiny, sparkling Nativity Fairies. Through the years, these fairies migrated across the nations to spread the light of the gospel in the hearts of every living thing. On Christmas eve, in the woods and in the mountains, in the sea and in the sky, all living creatures bow wing, knee, paw, and hoof to give honor to the king of all kings.

NEW YEAR'S

I am often told by the Prince of Fairies that no human has ever seen the New Year fairies because they are more secretive than the others. There are two tribes of New Year fairies. One tribe lives deep within the core of the Earth and spends 364 days tunneling back and forth. They are very serious about their work. The other tribe lives in the Sun. Fairies celebrate New Year's Eve during the Winter Solstice—the longest night of the year.

This is usually a few days before Christmas. The earth moves very slowly during the Winter Solstice, which allows a Sun fairy to fly to earth's highest point. If someone stood outside and looked at the sky during the Winter Solstice, they might see the Sun fairy, but they would assume it was a falling star. The Sun fairy brings a piece of the star, burning and blazing, to the top of Mount Everest, a location not pestered with many humans, where he or she delivers the hot shard of iron to the waiting New Year Fairy. The New Year Fairy passes the hot coal down deep through the fairy tunnels to the Earth's core. Thus, the core of our planet is refreshed with new fire from the Sun.

WINTER

February has several holiday fairies associated with it. Many people don't like February, but I think the month is misunderstood. February is cold and gray on the outside but candy-apple red and filled with the warmth of love at heart—not just romantic love, but compassion and kindness. Under that cold grayness of winter is the hope of sleeping flower bulbs that dream of creeping back up through the soil to feel sunshine on their "faces." Down deep in the earth, the spring colors are resting and waiting. Above that cold grayness are the secret chambers of the warm breezes that pull on the reins of nature like horses anticipating a race; these winds wait impatiently in their holding place, chatting of kites, butterflies, and birdsong.

We know that February second is Groundhog's Day. This is a particular favorite of mine since it is also my birthday. Every groundhog has a special fairy assigned to it. Groundhogs are amazing creatures. When they are working, or digging, they work and dig hard. When they are sleeping, or hibernating, they sleep deep and long. The Groundhog Fairy is responsible for making sure that the groundhog wakes up just after sunrise on his special day to predict the coming of an early spring or a late winter. In the wild places, when the groundhog emerges from his den (prodded by its special furry fairy), it will find quite an assembly of

fairies and animal creatures waiting for the weather news. This day is extremely important to fairies who work with dryads to prepare for blooming and migration.

February second is also Candlemas Day. It marks the midpoint of winter. On Candlemas Day, many ground-dwelling tribes of fairies (including the woodland fairies and the deep valley fairies) celebrate by lighting tiny candles outside their earthen lairs. I witnessed the beauty of Candlemas once when I was hiking along a stream deep in a deciduous wood at sunset. As I observed my surroundings, I watched as thousands of tiny lights began to glow along the slopes and hills on either side of the stream. At first I believed it to be glow worms, but upon investigation I found tiny little beeswax candles flickering.

Valentine's Day is definitely an enchanted holiday. It brings to mind different things to different people. To me, Valentine's Day has always been a time to give a token to those you love to remind them that they are special. The day is filled with purple-velvety fairies. When I was a child, the Valentine fairies taught me how to change a shoebox into a magical Valentine's mailbox where all my classmates would drop little Valentine's cards and candies selected just for me. The candy that one received for Valentine's was so special. The Valentine fairies shared fey recipes to select candy makers. If you ever taste this candy, you will know it. Your eyes will close and you will hum an unknown tune as tribute to the candy's enchanted flavor. Love is shown in tiny gifts given from the heart. My daddy has a tradition that was inspired by the wee purple folk. He purchases every lady in our family a special box of Valentine chocolates. I have a large curio in my family room where I keep almost every heart-shaped box that daddy has given me over my lifetime on display. To look at it is to see the kindness of my wonderful father and to remember the loving fairies.

The Valentine or February fairies are incredibly talented. Some are icicle makers. It rarely snows where I live in Alabama, however, one cold February

day everything was covered in snow. I saw a shimmer of light in the branches of a cedar tree. A winter fairy was shedding her shadow! As the shadow fell to the snowy ground it froze and I quickly gathered it. It didn't melt but transformed into something similar to sparkling mica dust. I still have this little glittery ice shadow in my chest of treasures.

Some winter fairies have the power to wake the sleeping flower bulbs to bring laughing tulips and dancing daffodils into our lives. Others spend most of February waking up the sleepy deciduous tree dryads to prepare them for March and leaf budding.

A pooka grazes peacefully
where the river
meets the sea
In the ruins of a castle,
watched by me.
A moment of enchantment
where the city meets the green
and I enjoy the magic
as I watch, unseen.

— Geraldine M. Byrne

7

Pookas

Have you ever had the feeling that something is watching you? Especially when you stroll through a flower garden or along a wooded trail? I don't mean the normal feeling of fairy eyes and wildlife peering out at you from hiding spots. I mean the feeling that even your thoughts are loud enough to be heard. If you understand this feeling, you were probably walking side by side with a kind-hearted Pooka. Long ago when all the land was still filled with ancient trees and clean rivers, the teddy bear-like Pookas flourished. As mankind spread across the land, the Pookas decided to become invisible. They only occasionally show themselves to people. Pookas choose when and where they are visible. They also choose their shape and appearance.

All Pookas have pointed ears so that they can hear even the softest sounds (sometimes even our thoughts) and they have sensitive noses so they can sniff out faint scents (especially chocolate). Pookas can see in the dark. Most Pookas are fur-covered from the tips of their ears to the tips of their toes. They are extremely cuddly. Have you ever been in your bed at night feeling afraid of the dark when suddenly you felt warm and cozy? Your eyes got heavy and you drifted off into sweet dreams? If so, this means a Pooka crept into your covers and snuggled you close to take care of you through the dark night.

There are many legends about Pookas. In Ireland, a Pooka is a shapeshifter and can take any form it chooses, but usually it is seen in the form of a small animal such as a rabbit, dog, or goat. Sometimes they appear as ancient old men or women. Sometimes a Pooka is seen as a black horse with a wild flowing mane and shining golden eyes.

In the Southeastern United States, Pookas often appear as black bears, mountain lions, or golden eagles. Some folks around Alabama's Cheaha State Park believe there is a Pooka in the form of "Bigfoot" or "Sasquatch" living on their mountain!

An important thing to remember about Pookas is that they have the power of human speech. Sometimes they become very mischievous to make sport of a person who deserves it . They have been known to embellish the truth—that is, they are GOOD liars and tricky!

When I was a little girl, I had a Pooka friend. His name was Noseplips. One February he appeared at my third birthday party. I was eating chocolate cake and he walked right up to me, bowed like a gentleman, and asked, "Might I have a slice of that delicious concoction?" I giggled and gave him my plate. From that moment on, he was my best friend. He was a little taller than I was and covered in purple fur. But he could become very big and make me feel safe! His face looked like a bit like a rabbit, with a teddy bear body and a fuzzy purple beard. Noseplips went everywhere with me. My mom even set a plate at the dinner table for him, although she could not see him. He taught me my colors, the alphabet, and how to draw pigs by connecting the letters E, M, W, W, O, and S. I will show you how to do this if you attend one of my fairy workshops. Noseplips was fascinated with pigs, especially chocolate or candy pigs.

No one else could see Noseplips. My mom was a little worried about my "invisible friend" and took the five-year-old me to my pediatrician for a checkup. Dr. Luther (whom you may have read about in my first book, *Calico Ghosts*) simply grinned as she peered over her spectacles at my mother. She said, "Renee has an imaginary playmate. Most extremely bright children do have one of these during their childhood. Don't worry, Mrs. Simmons. I'm certain Noseplips will have to depart someday to go play with another child who needs him." Needless to say, I wasn't really happy with Dr. Luther's explanation, because I knew Noseplips would NEVER leave me. Ever!

One summer day when I was six, Noseplips and I were having a picnic under the Grandpop Tree in Granddad's meadow. We had finished drinking purple Kool-Aid and had eaten all of our cheese squares when he announced rather sadly, "I must away."

I didn't understand him. For the past three years, Noseplips had come and gone unannounced. But he was always around . . . somewhere. He explained that Dr. Luther had been right. It was time for him to go. He would always love me, but another little girl needed him. I didn't want to cry, but a few tears sneaked down my cheeks. We hugged, I gave Noseplips the whole chocolate candy pig that we had planned to share, and he became invisible.

I've never seen Noseplips again, but I have caught glimpses of purple fur out of the corner of my eye, and I think he still drops in occasionally to check on me. Perhaps when I am a silly old woman he will come back for a picnic and we will drink purple Kool-Aid and share a chocolate pig once again!

Don't be surprised if someday, as you walk along in your garden or through the woods, you meet an animal walking on hind legs, possibly wearing a top hat, who can talk to you in your own language.

There are many other stories I could tell you and many other creatures I would like to introduce to you. But I must *away now* myself. I need to build a few more fairy houses and chat with our willow tree about the lovely purple violets growing across her roots.

Twalah!

Activities

CHAPTER 1—

Go for a family walk when the moon is full. A whole new set of animals, sights, and sounds waits to be discovered in the moonlight. Listen to animal sounds and movements in the shadows. Owls and bats are hunting their prey. Watch for glowing things, like worms, fireflies, and fungus on trees. And remember to look up at the stars!

Help your child discover a hidden universe. Find a scrap board (maybe two feet by two feet) and place it on bare dirt in your backyard. Come back in a day or two, lift the board, and see how many species have found shelter there. Identify these creatures with the help of a field guide. Return to this universe once a month, lift the board and discover who's new.

Tell stories to your children about your special childhood places in nature. Did you have a fort? A tree house? A special rock? Then help them find their own unique place: leaves beneath a backyard willow, the bend of a creek, or a meadow in the woods. Let it become their intimate connecting place with the natural world. If they don't have access to nature, bring it to them! Help them create a terrarium for their room or a small flower/vegetable garden on a patio.

Revive old traditions. Capture lightning bugs at dusk, release them at dawn. Make a leaf collection. Paint a picture of a lovely forest or meadow. Keep a terrarium or aquarium.

Invent your own nature game. Help your kids pay attention during hikes or easy walks by playing 'find ten critters'—mammals, birds, insects, reptiles, snails, and other creatures. Finding a critter can also mean discovering footprints, mole holes, and other signs that an animal has passed by or lives there.

CHAPTER 2—

Books to read (if you are serious about becoming a fairy expert):

Peter Pan and *Peter and Wendy: The Boy Who Wouldn't Grow Up* (J. M. Barrie).

The Coming of the Fairies (Sir Arthur Conan Doyle).

Fairy Tales and Fantasy Stories (Louisa May Alcott).

The Spiderwick Chronicles series (Tony DiTerlizzi and Holly Black).

The Cherokee Little People (Marijo Moore and Emma Shaw-Smith).

The Deetkatoo: Native American Stories about Little People (John Bierhorst).

Plan a nature vacation. There are many options! If you really want to get close to the world of the wee folk, go camping in a state park. Hike the trails. Wade in the creeks and streams. Watch for tiny wet footprints on the rocks. Build fairy houses near your campsite. Sleep in a tent, or better yet, a hammock! Listen for the sounds of fairies: laughter, tinkling bells, and whispers in the treetops.

CHAPTER 3—
Building Fairy Houses

Fairy houses are tiny constructed homes for the fairies and nature's friends to visit. Twigs, sticks, tree bark, dry grasses, polished pebbles, shells, found feathers, moss, pine cones, and nuts are a few of the items that can be used. Ranging from rustic to intricate, these enchanting habitats are built by children, families, gardeners and nature lovers reflecting their creativity, joy and pride. The simple challenge of creating a home for a fairy gives children a unique activity that encourages them to play outside and connect with the natural world, nurturing care and respect for the environment while feeding the imagination.

Ask the child to hold up his or her pointing finger. Encourage them to imagine that they are the same size as that finger. Where would they live? What would they need in their habitat?

Fairy houses can take many forms and can be created in many different places. Find a quiet place away from roads or busy pathways. The base of a tree or to the side of a rock could be just right. Close to the ground is usually best. Sometimes you may find a special place in the low branches of a tree or bush. Many fairy houses look so natural that they are almost hidden.

Steps for Building

Allow the children (working in small groups or individually) to select a safe location for their house.

Encourage children to gather natural materials from the area (without disturbing living things).

Allow the builder(s) to tour you through their creation(s). Adults are amazed at the imagination revealed during these tours. Take close-up photographs of each house and photos of each with the builders sitting next to the house.

If possible, revisit the fairy house the day after construction. Look for "visitors" such as ants, frogs, bees, dragonflies, ladybugs, etc. These little creatures are fairy spies sent to investigate the houses to see if the fairies might want to visit. Often there is some "damage" to the house; children will usually explain that the damage is due to a fairy visit during the night.

Sometimes the fairies have left tokens of appreciation behind for the child to find on the next visit. Look closely for such items. It is not guaranteed that tokens will be left, but it is fun to hope!

Creating Fairy Lures to Attract the Fairies

Fairy lures are whimsical "wind mobile" type hangings made from natural materials, string, and items that you collect. The purpose is not to catch a fairy, but to catch a fairy's attention as it flies by and to indicate that there are fairy houses nearby. Some of the items dangling from my lures are old silver spoons, beads, prisms from a broken chandelier, charms, and other cherished tokens. Remember to place fairy lures only in your own garden or forest—we don't want to use any unnatural items on public lands because they could become litter.

CHAPTER 4—

Become friends with the seasons, spring, summer, fall, and winter—each is so unique and beautiful. Use your observation skills to notice the sky, clouds, sun patterns, night stars, and changes in plants and animals.

Keep a seasonal journal of the weather, clouds, animals, and plants that you see. Make it unique by drawing pictures, writing poems and stories, and adding notes about what you like to do during that season.

My father told me a story, "Brother Leaf," when I was a little girl. I share this story during my autumn storytelling programs. It is about a Native American boy who wanted to walk among the animals without frightening them. The trees created a leaf mask for the boy so that he was invisible when he wore the mask. One day after he had helped many animals and had their trust, the mask was removed and he could walk among the creatures of the forest as himself.

Make a leaf mask and wear it into the forest. See

if you can look deeper at the wild places through the mask.

CHAPTER 5—

Read the *Narnia* series by C. S. Lewis. The movies are enchanting as well, but always read the books first!

Choose a "favorite" tree and really get to know that tree. Not just the natural history of the tree. Sit on its roots or in its limbs. Listen, smell and feel the life in and around the tree. Talk to the tree. Tell it stories. Perhaps it might become comfortable enough with you to answer! You can keep a tree-sitting journal and write down all the things you observe and the stories of the tree. Then create your own fairy tales.

Research and study the unique plants in your environment. They are amazing! Find out which plants are edible or medicinal. Create a garden in your own yard. If you don't have a yard, you can have plants on a windowsill or ask your neighbors to help create a community garden.

CHAPTER 6—

Mirror spying game: Fairies and elves tend NOT to look at themselves in mirrors so they don't pay special attention to reflections. Keep a small mirror nearby (mine is a pendant on a chain round my neck) and every now and again use the mirror to look behind you—you may catch a glimpse of a fairy, elf, or gnome moving about!

Create special holiday fairy houses: a nest in your Christmas tree, a carved pumpkin, a Candlemas Feast table set under an old tree. Use your imagination!

Valentine's Fairy Tea: Invite your friends over for a special tea party with a fairy theme. Celebrate winter and friendship with a cozy tea party underneath a tent of quilts or beside your flaming fireplace. Create "secret fairy" Valentine cards that you and your friends leave for people who might need a bit of cheer during the winter months.

CHAPTER 7—

Watch the movie *Harvey* (written by Mary Chase

and starring Jimmy Stewart) and have a Pooka Picnic on Pooka Day, which is November 1st in Ireland but the first of ANY month in the United States and Canada.

The late Katherine Tucker Windham, a friend and incredible storyteller, always cried "Rabbit! Rabbit!" on the first day of every month to bring good luck and to keep the Pookas happy.

Pookas love dyed boiled eggs (similar to Easter Eggs), so you may want to have a decorated egg hunt during your picnic as well. The person who finds the most eggs wins a chocolate pig, of course! And don't worry if you can't find a chocolate pig. Any chocolate will do just fine.

If a child is to keep alive his inborn sense of wonder without any such gift from the fairies, he needs the companionship of at least one adult who can share it, rediscovering with him the joy, excitement and mystery of the world we live in.

— Rachel Carson

No child but must remember laying his head in the grass, staring into the infinitesimal forest and seeing it grow populous with fairy armies.

— Robert Louis Stevenson,
Essays in the Art of Writing

Resources for Teachers and Educators

Expanded Activity: Building Fairy Houses and Enhancing Observation Skills

What Is a Fairy House?

Fairy houses are tiny constructed homes for the fairies and nature's friends to visit. Twigs, tree bark, dry grasses, little pebbles, dried shells, naturally shed feathers, dried seaweed, pine cones, and nuts are a few of the items that can be used. Ranging from rustic to intricate "fairy mansions," these enchanting habitats are built by children, families, gardeners and nature lovers reflecting their creativity, joy, and pride. The simple challenge of creating a home for a fairy gives children a unique activity that encourages them to go outside and connect with the natural world, nurturing care and respect for the environment. Some, like Dr. Richard Louv, would say this activity grants children a healthy dose of Vitamin N—nature!

CONCEPT:

The activity of building fairy houses offers unique opportunities for education. While children are fully engaged with building a fairy house they are stimulated in many ways—creating, observing, collecting, exercising, communicating and imagining—all while having lots of fun. It's a win-win situation for child *and* educator. Expanded environmental education will also help boost academic achievement. A number of studies have found that students who take part in environmentally themed lessons perform better in science and other subjects.

OBJECTIVES:

Encourage children (and parents) to get kids outside and connected with nature; provide a catalyst for curiosity; teach focus skills and methods of creative processing; enhance communication skills; improve teamwork skills.

SUPPLIES:

Use only natural materials and be respectful to living things (such as ferns, moss, flowers, etc)—fairies are careful not to harm living things.

Simple Activity: Children use ONLY what they find in the area selected for building fairy houses

Enhanced Activity: Children bring a small bag of their own unique natural materials (feathers, shells, clay, seeds, dried flowers, picked garden flowers, etc.) from home, or educator supplies "enhancement" objects to group.

LOCATION:

Fairy houses can take many forms and can be created in many different places. Find a quiet place away from roads or busy pathways. The base of a tree or the side of a rock could be just right. Close to the ground is usually best. Sometimes you may find a special place in the low branches of a tree or bush. Many fairy houses look so natural that they are almost hidden.

Extensions:

CREATIVE WRITING:

Letters to fairies; poetry; plays; descriptive essays (a popular theme is "What happened when the fairies visited my house . . .")

MATH: Graphs, measurements, shapes.

SCIENCE:

Research the objects that were found and used as part of the fairy house; research the creature visitors who visited the houses; identify the types of trees, rocks, plants, etc., in the area where the houses are built.

ART:

Drawing, collages, photography, sculpting, architectural design, construction, and balance.

Wind chimes in your yard will serenade garden creatures—squirrels, fairies and angels. It's easy to believe in magic when you're young. Anything you couldn't explain was magic then. It didn't matter if it was science or a fairy tale. Electricity and elves were both infinitely mysterious and equally possible—elves probably more so.

— Charles de Lint

A scientist in his laboratory is not a mere technician: he is also a child confronting natural phenomena that impress him as though they were fairy tales.

— Marie Curie

A National Problem

"Let's Move Outside" is a federal program designed to help children become healthier and more involved in nature and outdoor activities. It highlights a national recognition of problems with childhood obesity and their disconnect with the outdoors. Richard Louv's book *Last Child in the Woods* concludes that many children today are alienated from nature, suffering from what he terms "nature-deficit disorder."

When Louv interviewed my son in 2008 for his book, *Got Dirt? Beyond the Nature Deficit Disorder*, he said, "Teenager Josh Morrison founded GEEKs in the Woods for his friends and fellow geeks everywhere. He defines 'geek' as a 'gaming environmentally educated kid,' and says he and his friends—'tired of being labeled' tech addicts—can have their electronic games and their outdoor time, too: 'We could be the generation that makes a U-turn back to . . . a balance between virtual reality and what sustains all life . . . nature.'"

Joshua and my other son, Jo, were taught to build fairy houses practically from birth and have taught hundreds of their peers this hobby. Building fairy houses offers a unique remedy for nature disconnect through an activity that inspires an appreciation of the environment and expands imagination and creativity.

Educator Comments

What do I see in my students' sparkling eyes during the fairy houses activity? I see pride, excitement, learning and fun!

— Fourth Grade Teacher

Renee's stories and the activity of creating fairy habitats engage children's imaginations and rekindle interest in the natural world. A pine cone becomes a tree, pieces of bark become a roof, a shell becomes a bathtub, acorn caps become dishes. Will they get a visitor? Perhaps a chipmunk, frog or butterfly . . . and of course the potential for fairy guests!

— First Grade Teacher

The students enjoyed the activity immensely. The only issue we had was getting them to STOP creating. It is a rare thing to see K-6 graders so involved in something that is not related to electronics.

— Elementary School Principal

We built our fairy village in our outdoor classroom area over a period of six weeks. Every day we'd take a few minutes to work on the houses, improve and enhance them, or repair small damage done in the night (by the fairies that used them, of course). During this time the students wrote letters to the fairies in a journal. We noticed an increase in the students' concentration skills and their overall grades improved.

— Sixth Grade Teacher

Fairy House programs have inspired an enormous variety of activities in our school, including nature walks, artwork, sorting, creative drama, collecting, reading, writing, math and science activities, web browsing, and best of all, cooperating! I am still hearing fairy house stories every day from students, parents and teachers!

— Media Specialist

K-5 Curriculum Support

Hairy, Scary, but Mostly Merry Fairies! and Nature Observation through Fairy Houses workshops support a curriculum for Science, Literature, Oral and Visual Communication, and Extended Standards K-5:

KINDERGARTEN CONTENT

Earth & Space Science

10. Identify objects observed in the day sky with the unaided eye, including the sun, clouds, moon, and rainbows.

Objective K.10.1: Identify the sun and clouds in the day sky.

Objective K.10.2: Describe a rainbow.

First Grade Content

Literature

6. Recognize a variety of narrative text forms, including fairy tales, adventure stories, and poetry.

- Identify characters, settings, problems, and solutions in a variety of texts.
- Compare story elements through text-to-text connections.

7. Use the basic features of informational text to distinguish fact from fiction.

Examples: captions, headings, table of contents.

Writing & Language

8. Use complete sentences to address a topic or tell a story.

- Use graphic organizers to outline content.
- Reread to make revisions.
- Edit for spelling, punctuation, and capitalization.
- Publish final draft.
- Use descriptive, narrative, and expository modes of writing.

- Write simple poems addressing a topic.

Research & Inquiry

12. Collect information from print and nonprint resources to investigate a teacher- or student-selected topic.

Examples: nonfiction books, videos, resource persons, interviews, Web-based sources, dictionaries.

- Generate oral and written questions to gather information.
- Use parts of a book to locate information.
- Use alphabetical order to the first letter to access information.
- Interpret information from simple charts, maps, graphs, and directions.

Oral & Visual Communication

13. Listen for meaning in conversations and discussions, including looking at the speaker without interrupting.

- Follow two- and three-part oral directions.
- Make connections to literature read aloud.

Examples: text-to-text, text-to-self,

text-to-world.

14. Use appropriate intonation when speaking and interacting with others.

- Use grammar and word choice appropriate for a specific audience.
- Recite poems, rhymes, songs, and stories.
- Demonstrate the ability to take turns in a conversation.
- Expand vocabulary reflective of a growing range of interests and knowledge.
- Use pictures, objects, music, and computer resources to present information.
- Use the writing process to prepare oral presentations.

Physical Science

2. Identify basic properties of objects.

EXAMPLES: size, shape, color, texture

Objective 1.2.1: Describe the shape, size, and texture of objects using the terms *big*, *little*, *soft*, *hard*, *round*, *square*, *rough*, and *smooth*.

Objective 1.2.2: Classify objects according to size.

Objective 1.2.3: Classify objects according to color.

Life Science

4. Describe survival traits of living things, including color, shape, size, texture, and covering.

Objective 1.4.1: List ways plants and animals protect themselves.

Objective 1.4.2: Identify basic needs of plants and animals, including air, water, food, and shelter.

Objective 1.4.3: Categorize plants and animals by color, shape, size, texture, and covering.

Additional content to be taught:

- Classify plants and animals according to physical traits.

  EXAMPLES: animals—six legs on insects, plants—green leaves on evergreen trees.

- Identify developmental stages of plants and animals.

  EXAMPLES: plants—seed developing into seedling, seedling developing into tree; animals—piglet developing into pig, kid developing into goat.

- Describe a variety of habitats and natural homes of animals.

Earth & Space Science

7. Identify components of Earth's surface, including soil, rocks, and water.

Objective 1.7.1: Differentiate between soil and rocks.

Objective 1.7.2: Illustrate components of Earth's surface, including soil, rocks, and water.

8. Recognize daily changes in weather, including clouds, precipitation, and temperature.

Objective 1.8.1: Define precipitation and temperature.

Objective 1.8.2: Identify rain, snow, and hail as forms of precipitation.

Objective 1.8.3: Identify appropriate clothing for different types of weather.

Objective 1.8.4: Describe seasonal changes in the weather.

Additional content to be taught:

- Recognize instruments to observe weather.
  EXAMPLES: thermometer, rain gauge, wind

sock, weather vane.

- Record weather data using weather journals, charts, and maps.

9. Identify ways to conserve Earth's resources.

Example: turn off lights and water when not in use

Objective 1.9.1: Define *conserve*.

Objective 1.9.2: Identify the sun, water, and wind as examples of Earth's resources.

10. Describe uses of recycled materials.

Examples: manufacture of paper products from old newspapers, production of mulch from trees.

Objective 1.10.1: Define *recycle*.

Objective 1.10.2: List materials that can be recycled.

11. Compare the day sky to the night sky as observed with the unaided eye.

Objective 1.11.1: Identify the moon and stars as objects in the night sky.

Objective 1.11.2: Identify the sun, clouds, and rainbows as objects in the day sky.

Second Grade

Literature

6. Differentiate among folktales, tall tales, fables, realistic fiction, and other narrative texts.

- Recognize the author's purpose or intent in a variety of texts.
- Infer the main idea and supporting details in narrative texts.
- Summarize the plot and characters' actions and motivations in narrative texts.
- Recognize morals and lessons in narrative texts.

Writing & Language

8. Organize sentences into a paragraph to address a topic or tell a story.

- Sort information using graphic organizers.
- Generate a topic sentence and a concluding sentence in a paragraph.
- Draft a written piece, including an introductory paragraph and a concluding paragraph.
- Edit for spelling, punctuation,

capitalization, and sentence variety.

- Publish final draft.
- Use descriptive, narrative, and expository modes of writing.
- Write free verse poetry to express ideas.

Oral & Visual Communication

14. Respond to various types of literature read aloud.

- Focus attention on a speaker without interrupting.
- Follow multistep oral directions.
- Interpret presented information.

15. Select appropriate voice tone, gestures, and facial expression to enhance meaning.

- Use active listening skills.
  Example: "Stop, Look, and Listen" technique.
- Retell stories and events in logical order.
- Remain on topic when speaking.
- Use visual aids, props, and technology in oral presentations.
  Examples: poster, puppet, slideshow.

- Use appropriate grammar and word choice in oral presentations and in conversations.

Physical Science

2. Identify vibration as the source of sound.

Objective 2.2.1: Relate a variety of sounds to their sources, including weather, animal, and transportation sounds.

Objective 2.2.2: Identify different sounds produced by vibrations in the environment.

> EXAMPLES: rustling sound of leaves caused by blowing wind, buzzing sound of bees caused by rapid wing movement, whirring sound of helicopters caused by rotation of propellers.

Additional content to be taught:

- Identify pitch and volume as properties of sound.
- Distinguish between pitch and volume of sound.

Life Science

5. Identify the relationship of structure to function in plants, including roots, stems, leaves, and flowers.

Objective 2.5.1: Identify plant roots, stems, leaves, and flowers, including how they benefit the plant.

Objective 2.5.2: Identify plant needs for growth.

6. Identify characteristics of animals, including behavior, size, and body covering.

Objective 2.6.1: Identify animal behaviors and characteristics that help them survive.

Objective 2.6.2: Describe physical traits of animals, including color, shape, and size.

Additional content to be taught:

- Compare existing animals to extinct animals.

  Examples: iguana to stegosaurus, elephant to wooly mammoth.

- Identify migration and hibernation as survival strategies.

Third Grade

Literature

5. Compare poetry, folktales, and fables in respect to their genre characteristics.

6. Recognize linguistic and cultural similarities and differences in multicultural literature.

   Examples: regional dialects, clothing, food, games.

7. Compare fictional characters and events to real-life experiences.

   Example: relate hardships faced by early settlers in literature to hardships faced by families today.

8. Use text features to guide interpretation of expository texts, including italics, headings, maps, and charts.

   Examples: social studies—locate physical features on a map; science—interpret weather data from charts and tables.

- Interpret the author's purpose or intent in a given text.

Oral and Visual Communication

13. Demonstrate the ability to follow multistep oral directions.

14. Demonstrate eye contact, articulation, and appropriate voice intonation with oral narrative presentations.

- Use dramatizations with oral descriptive presentations.
- Use figurative language to enhance oral communication.

  EXAMPLES: simile, onomatopoeia, metaphor, alliteration.
- Utilize precise vocabulary in oral presentations.

  EXAMPLES: *exceptional* instead of *good*, *brilliant* instead of *smart*.

Fourth Grade

Oral and Visual Communication

13. Demonstrate eye contact, articulation, and appropriate voice intonation with descriptive presentations.

- Use demonstrations with oral expository presentations.
- Use figurative language to enhance oral communication.

  Examples: simile, metaphor, onomatopoeia, personification.
- Utilize precise vocabulary in oral presentations.

  Examples: *leap* instead of *jump*, *miniature* instead of *little*.

14. Identify strategies of a skillful listener, including attending to the listening task and assigning meaning to the message.

FIFTH GRADE

Oral & Visual Communication

12. Demonstrate eye contact, articulation, and appropriate voice intonation with expository presentations.

- Use dramatizations with oral persuasive presentations.

  EXAMPLES: role play, Reader's Theater.

- Use figurative language found in literature to enhance oral communication.

  EXAMPLES: personification, idiom, metaphor, simile, hyperbole, onomatopoeia, alliteration, symbolism.

13. Apply strategies of a skillful listener, including maintaining eye contact, attending to the listening task, and assigning meaning to the message.

Always Remember . . .

A FAIRY MAY BE NEARBY IF YOU . . .

. . . observe that you are being followed by a titmouse or a chickadee.

. . . find large patches of four-leaf clovers.

. . . stumble upon a fairy mushroom ring.

. . . see a tiny whirlwind of leaves swirling across the forest floor.

. . . smell a sweet fragrance on the breeze.

. . . hear a soft chiming of bells, rustle of wings, or mysterious giggles.

. . . sense that someone is watching you.